© 2020 Ky Ston Distribution, All Rights Reserved

ISBN; paperback 978-1-7349715-4-5

All rights reserved. No part of this book may be reproduced or transmitted in any form or by any means, electronic or mechanical, including photocopying, recording, or by any information storage and retrieval system, without permission in writing from the copyright owner.

This book was printed in the United States of America

Contact:

P.O. Box 78443
Los Angeles, CA 90016

Book Inquiries:
1-888-614-6867

www.kystonbooks.com

Printed in the United States of America
9 8 7 6 5 4 3 2 1

Life Is Like A Traffic Light

ABOUT THE AUTHOR

I was inspired to write this book after reading the popular book *Who Moved My Cheese* by Dr. Spencer Johnson.

During the Coronavirus pandemic of 2020, most, if not all, of us have had to re-evaluate our lives and make some kind of adjustment to adapt to our "new normal". Prior to the pandemic we moved as we pleased. We dined indoors at restaurants, hugged loved ones and socialized freely with friends. Those days are over – at least for the time being. Today, we're forced to pause and change course – the light is no longer GREEN.

Life Is Like A Traffic Light

These Examples Relate to Us All

Sometimes we as human beings make life more complicated than it needs to be. Following three simple principles to guide our lives can make the journey so much more enlightening.

Life's journey consists of three distinct components:

We're born.

We live.

We die.

The traffic light is our guide.

When the light is green in our lives, we have the right to proceed in doing the things we want, need and desire to do. When the light turns yellow it's time to slow down and not be hurried. And of course, when the light turns red, we must cease everything. All must come to a complete

Life Is Like A Traffic Light

stop. We must be still and evaluate what is meaningful in our lives. It's a perfect time to reflect until the next green light.

Grasping these three simple concepts can change our perception of the experiences we encounter. Having an awareness of, and appreciation for, the principles and components illustrated here can aid in the development or enhancement of our humility and empathy for humankind.

We are all in different phases of life's journey, intersecting at various points. In an ideal world, as our paths cross, we're met with respect, compassion and love. But sadly, discrimination and hate create obstacles that negatively impact us all.

Life Is Like A Traffic Light

DEDICATION

This book is dedicated to everyone who has suffered as they attempt to create a better life for themselves and their families; those who haven't achieved their goal but refuse to give up; those among us living in the red with few or no opportunities for yellow or green experiences and those living life in the fast lane who can't or refuse to slow down.

Life Is Like A Traffic Light

The Meaning of Green Light

To start.
Make it happen.
Don't wait for anyone.
No time for sleeping.
Proceed.

Life Is Like A Traffic Light

The Green Light

Remember life as a youth? The basics of the game red light, green light many of us played? It was so much fun back in the day. For those who aren't familiar – allow me to enlighten you. One person is chosen to be "It" (the traffic light) and he/she stands a good distance away from the other players with his/her back to them. The other players stand in a line facing "It". When they call out "green light," the players in line move toward "It" until he/she spins around, calling "red light." Any player still moving is out of the game. The game teaches a simple but important lesson: when to proceed (go) and when to cease (stop).

Every day seemed to be a green light experience for us as kids. We were free to go to the neighborhood park, the corner store

Life Is Like A Traffic Light

and visit friends. Some of the best times were when a group of us would ride the local bus to the mall, to the movies and to get food that we often shared. It was "let's go, let's eat, let's play"—a constant pace of "go". There appeared to be nothing in the way of our going, no *reason* to stop. We had no sense of time. When you're young you take chances and risks and, sometimes, defy authority. If the worst thing to happen was a spanking or a punishment that lasted a few hours, it would be worth it.

Once I became a young adult, I began to notice things changing around me. It was during that time that I recall my father sitting me down to have, what I came to see, as our first adult-to-adult conversation. I didn't know what to expect. My father's tone and facial expression were extremely serious, unlike any other time I could recall. For the past 18 years I had lived my life as a kid and now all of a sudden, I was being

Life Is Like A Traffic Light

approached as a young man.

The conversation went a little like this: "Son, it's time for you and me to have a talk. You just turned eighteen and now things must change here in this household."

Dumbfounded, I asked, "Things like what?"

"For starters, you need to find yourself a job and contribute. If you want to continue to live in my house, you must pay your way by helping with the bills of the house."

I was clueless. "Where would I find a job? I don't know what I qualify for; I have no experience. Besides, I just turned eighteen *yesterday*. Don't I have a few months?" I asked.

"No, you don't have a few months. It's time to grow up and take on adult responsibilities."

"I don't want to grow up and I don't want to take on responsibilities. Can I just be a kid?" I asked.

"Son, you are no longer a kid. Those days are

Life Is Like A Traffic Light

over. Turning eighteen places you in a different category. When you turn twenty-one you will be placed in another category."

"What category is twenty-one?" I asked, as I sat there with my heart racing.

"Turning twenty-one makes you legal. That means you can purchase liquor and you can drink. You will be able to go to Las Vegas and gamble if you choose to. You will be considered a full-grown man. Oh, you will then have rent to pay, utilities, car notes, and auto insurance; you have to buy your own food and get a 40-hour a week job to support yourself," my father answered.

This took the air right out of my lungs. I was left breathless for a moment as I formulated my next question. My father stood up, placed his hands behind his back and tilted his head to the right, waiting for me to say something. "Well?"

"Well, what?" I answered.

Life Is Like A Traffic Light

"Well, did you understand what I just said to you?"

"Yes. I have to take it all in and digest everything."

"It's time to go out into the world and see what the real world feels like. You're only able to be a child for seventeen years. Your mother and I refuse to mollycoddle you. We are not equipped to let you live off of us until you're thirty or forty years old. If I allowed you to live off me for free, I would be a damn fool," said my father as he walked away.

I sat there for a few minutes before I got up to take a walk. While I was walking around the neighborhood, I couldn't help but think about what my father said to me. I related his words to the best metaphor my lingering adolescence could muster - "The light is green. Get moving."

As I thought about my life for the next couple of hours, I realized this world could be cold and

Life Is Like A Traffic Light

that I needed to prepare myself for hard knocks. Nothing in this world is free and nothing will be easy, and I'm not talking about just being a Black man living in America. I'm talking about being an *adult*. I started to fill out applications for jobs with little success due to lack of experience. I wanted to attend college but neither my parents nor I had any money to pay for it. Being the oldest of eight siblings, I knew my chances of going to college were slim because my mother was on welfare and my father decided to stop working after my mother gave birth to the last child. What a fine time to stop working, with a wife and eight children. My father and I entered into an agreement. I asked that he give me one year and I would be out of the house and would never return. He agreed.

Now I had two choices. Find a job that would pay my rent and bills or find a place to stay where my rent would be free until I could take

Life Is Like A Traffic Light

care of myself. Three days after my eighteenth birthday I began my mission. I continued to apply for local jobs at fast-food restaurants, hardware and grocery stores, and I made it my business to befriend people who might offer me a place to stay; otherwise, in twelve months I would be an eighteen-year-old homeless kid. That was the last thing I wanted for myself.

Once a week my mother and I would sit and have a mother-and-son conversation. She would ask me how things were going and how I was holding up. I explained to her that I was afraid of what my future would look like in twelve months and she would always say to me, "Where there's a will, there's a way. Have faith and believe everything will be all right. Fear nothing and keep your eyes and ears open for opportunities. They will come." I lived by my mother's encouraging words.

Nine months later I was sitting at a nearby

Life Is Like A Traffic Light

bus stop bench when a woman three times my age sat down beside me and struck up a conversation. We talked and laughed while she waited for the bus to arrive. We exchanged names and telephone numbers. We spoke every day and night.

One week before it was time for me to leave home, I still had not found a job or a place to stay. Making it worse, one afternoon my sisters and I were at Venice Beach when the youngest one spit in an older gentleman's face, and I slapped her. When we got back home – without delay – she told our father what I had done to her, but totally left out the reason why. Not pausing for a moment, my father approached and slapped me as hard he could. It was at that moment I packed my things and left.

I called the older woman I had been speaking to and shared my story with her. She offered me a place to stay, allowing me to move in with her

Life Is Like A Traffic Light

and her seven children. Interesting enough, her youngest child was nineteen and I was eighteen. I felt very uncomfortable with the arrangement but at this point I felt as though I had no other options. "Desperate people do desperate things." Just that quickly, my life had changed course without much notice. Of course, I had known I needed to find another place to live. but I had no idea that my father's actions would rock me to my core and cause me to abruptly flee the only home I knew. What I learned that day is that you must be ready at any given time for change. Change can be hard regardless of whether it's planned or hits when you least expect it.

During my stay at my new home, my lady friend taught me how to sew. Together we designed and made custom sweat suits for people in the neighborhood. We would require a deposit for fabric and material then, since neither of us had a car, we would ride the local

Life Is Like A Traffic Light

bus downtown to the garment district to shop. My job was to cut and prep the fabric while she sewed. On each of our sweat suits we would profit between $75 and $100. That was in 1978, when $100 was a lot of money and a dollar went much further than it does today. With the profit from our little home-based business, we were able to pay the household bills with money left to spare.

I was able to purchase a used 1976 Cadillac. I had a roof over my head, a car and a few dollars in my pocket. I wasn't rich by any means, but at nineteen years old, I felt like I was. It didn't take much to make me happy then. And now, in this pandemic, many of us have come to realize we don't need much, and the things we thought we *needed* were really just wants and desires. Today, all we truly need is to remain safe from this virus, food on our tables, a roof over our heads and to maintain some peace of mind.

Life Is Like A Traffic Light

When you're standing at a crosswalk or driving and come to a traffic light that turns green, it clearly means *go, move, get it rolling, don't stop*. But life isn't a vehicle and we don't live at a crosswalk or govern ourselves by illuminating traffic lights. If you're always on the go or on the move and moving fast, at some point you crash or are forced to come to a screeching halt. Your financial stability may take a dive; an accident that impacts your mobility may occur; or you become so distracted by the business of your life that the most important things are overlooked, taken for granted and ultimately lost.

The color green that symbolizes "proceed" is also associated with *life*.

So the next time you're sitting in traffic waiting for the light to turn, take a few minutes to think on these things and ask yourself:

1. What are my life's accomplishments?
2. Have I set and achieved goals for myself...

Life Is Like A Traffic Light

is there more?
3. Am I living my best life or am I wasting time?
4. What is my purpose?
5. How can I serve and help others?
6. Have I corrected my mistakes or righted the wrongs of my life?
7. What can I do to become a better person?

These are just a few simple things we should reflect on as we "go" through life. You must know where you have been in order to know where you want to go, even if you haven't been anywhere. Another thing I have learned and try to keep in mind, is that life comes with challenges that must be overcome in order to shape us into our better selves. If you give up or give in then those unfaced challenges will become your final destination. In life there will always something to fight for or against. You may find yourself

Life Is Like A Traffic Light

fighting for freedom, a promotion, love or just to stay alive. Oftentimes we need to fight against negative thoughts and messages that clutter our minds. There is only so much we can do alone, so we must surround ourselves with others who can and are willing to support and lift us up when faced with what could seem the fight of our life.

I took a moment to answer the seven questions above and here are my answers.

1. I have tried to do everything I ever thought about doing, including becoming a professional robot dancer and appearing on three television shows, to include the The Johnny Carson Show in 1980. I became a professional street hustler for a few months and purchased my first home in 1982. In 1985 I opened my first legitimate business in Inglewood, California. 1986 brought the opening of the first Black-owned nightclub in the city of Marina Del Rey, California and

Life Is Like A Traffic Light

I was granted a liquor license in my name at the young age of 28. In 1992 I was the first to open a home health care agency. A year later, at age 34, I built a $3 million mansion in Bel Air Crest overlooking the city. I wrote my first book in 1995, The Rollin' 80s, and sold 13,000 units without the assistance of internet or social media. Later that year, I opened a production company and prepared to produce my first feature film with F. Gary Gray as my Director. After several attempts to secure the funding needed to complete the film, I decided to give up and go back to writing. Over the next 10 years I wrote 39 books. Fast forward a bit – I have designed an animated cartoon, a board game, a card game for casinos and an online dating website. No matter where or when the idea struck, I put it on paper, began to research and went to work making dreams reality. I never allowed anyone to discourage me from achieving

Life Is Like A Traffic Light

my goals and only quit if it was a decision I came to on my own, having given it my all and determining for myself that it just wasn't going to happen.

2. When I look back on my life, I have achieved everything I wanted to without any regrets.

3. I have lived the best life I could live. One may ask, "What does that word really mean?" I can say I lived a fulfilled life, which included success and failure. I was never afraid of failing. You can't be afraid to try.

4. Today I know my true purpose for living. I used to feel that life was about acquiring "stuff" and being popular. Not today. Now, I strive to be kind to all. Love my neighbors and those I don't know. Help those in need. Share my wisdom with those who seek knowledge.

5. Life has truly been good to me. I have experienced what millions of people dreamed of. I have been near death and God stepped in

Life Is Like A Traffic Light

at the right time to save my life. I have a great relationship with two of my daughters and my grandchildren. I have found the love of my life, I have a few great friends and I'm healthy.

6. I have made two major mistakes in my time and I don't regret them. I have grown through those experiences. When you refuse to learn from your mistakes you tend to repeat them. Sometimes mistakes can cost you a little and sometimes they can cost you what may seem like everything. In 1993, I trusted the wrong employee and in 1994 I lost everything from one simple oversight. I had millions of dollars but no knowledge of how to protect what I owned. I left myself wide open to lose everything. If I had known to set up a trust and secure my property and money there, I would still have it all today. Lack of wisdom and knowledge can cause many to stumble. That is the one major mistake that cost me – literally and figuratively. Of course, the

Life Is Like A Traffic Light

one thing I never lost was the ability to re-start.
7. I started to listen to my friends and professionals who dealt in things I was unfamiliar with. I made it my business to do better and be better in my relationships and business. I had to learn that just because I had more "power" than someone else, didn't give me the right to mistreat them and/or measure their success against my own. Success comes and goes. I have had and not had. Material things don't define who you are in life. Those things are there to enjoy in the moment and, when you're done, put them away. This is not the case for relationships with family, friends or co-workers. You can't pick up a relationship on Monday, keep it for a few months and then throw it away. Real relationships aren't dispensable. They are meant to be treasured. For myself, when I began to read the Bible and understand God's word, I became a better person. I stopped judging people and

Life Is Like A Traffic Light

only passed judgment after they proved to be who they were. Today, I'm a better man because of what I have lost over the years, not what I've gained. The more I had, the bigger my head got and the farther my chest stood out. I believe that came from not having much growing up and not knowing how to deal with success when it came my way. Now that I understand the Gospel, I treat everyone the same without pre-judgment or discrimination. I'm a better person because I realize the meaning of "grace". Grace will humble your heart to find good in everyone.

As an exercise, let's take a moment to reflect on a few of the concepts that the color <u>green</u> is associated with: **Renewal**, *Energy*, *Growth* and *Safety*.

RENEWAL

In life it's okay to renew/re-direct your career path, renew/upgrade a car or renew/re-evaluate

Life Is Like A Traffic Light

the people you chose as friends after realizing the effort is not mutual or reciprocated. Sometimes we become complacent – at times to our detriment. We resist change. Instead of rocking the boat, some choose to stay in unhealthy work environments where they are disrespected and or discriminated against while others remain in abusive relationships with people who don't value or appreciate them.

ENERGY

In order to renew things or situations, sometimes you have to dig deep to find the energy to facilitate the change. Often though, the all-consuming business of work, family, school and everyday life can make it challenging to find the motivation to visualize, plan for and make such alterations. Especially today, many of us exhaust all the energy we have just coping with our new normal, the grief and pain of lives lost and the fear of the unknown.

Life Is Like A Traffic Light

GROWTH

Your growth comes from your experiences, mistakes, learning, changing, archiving, and becoming a new you. As I recounted previously, as a teenager I was asked to leave my parents' house when I turned eighteen. I was not prepared to grow up and face the world alone. I was frightened to death at the idea of becoming homeless or being murdered in the streets. It's so much easier to stay where you are than to face growth. Growth will take you places you could never imagine. Growing pains are real but inevitable. As we grow, so do our self- identity, beliefs and moral compass. These things help guide our path and are directly related to how we develop and navigate life.

SAFETY

One of the most important things we all desire for ourselves and our family is to be

Life Is Like A Traffic Light

safe when we are at home, at work or out in the world. Safety can sometimes come with a price – like a monthly fee for a home alarm service, health insurance or a reliable mode of transportation. Generally speaking, being mindful of our safety comes from learning to be more careful, to be aware of our surroundings and not to make assumptions about the intentions of those who cross our path.

As we "go" through life, at times we may find ourselves stuck in theoretical traffic. For example, there was an old man in an old, beat-up 1965 Chevy Impala. The car made lots of noise when in park, the window wouldn't go down, there was no heat or air conditioner, and the bucket seats needed to be upholstered. He had three old, bald tires and was in desperate need of a paint job.

One Friday evening during rush hour, the old man was stopped at a traffic light. He sat

Life Is Like A Traffic Light

there nervously because he knew he didn't have enough fuel to make it to the nearby gas station. When the light finally turned green the old man stepped on the gas...but his car gave out on him. He immediately put on his hazard lights, jumped out of the car and began to push it out of the street. It wasn't long before three other men joined in to help.

Just as the three strangers saw the old man struggling to remedy his situation and came to his aid, so too in life do we find that others may be ready and willing to assist us in working through our own trials. They are more likely to do so if they see you are already putting in the effort on your own.

It may be that the people in our lives refuse, or simply lack the capacity, to give us the gas we need to move forward in life and this can be a big source of disappointment in our lives. This is why it's important that we put time into

Life Is Like A Traffic Light

developing the fortitude to motivate *ourselves* to move through and beyond life's challenges and not to rely on others for the push we need.

So, get behind yourself and be your own cheerleader. When you're pushing yourself, you're moving in the direction you choose. If you rely on family or friends to provide you the gas you need could end up either stuck in the same place they found you or moving in the direction of those who refueled you.

We must be cautious, though, when living life in the green. While it can seem exciting, if there is no slowing down to reflect on where we've been and where we're going, we may miss opportunities to reevaluate or redirect. There are so many things I missed when I was living in the green. I had to *be* everywhere and *have* everything right then and there; no time to waste, no expense spared and no second thoughts given.

Life Is Like A Traffic Light

At the end of the day, not slowing down and never stopping to evaluate my life or take advice from others caused me to lose everything. I went from having millions of dollars to standing in line waiting to be approved for a welfare check and $196 EBT card. I used to hear people talking about Mike Tyson, the youngest heavy weight boxer in the world, blowing over $400 million during his fight career and later ending up broke. I understood all to clearly how you could go from having the world to having a street block. When we look back on Mike's life and lifestyle – he was always on the go: training, traveling, fighting, interviews, parties, etc.

    A green light will never change its own color. You have to make that change, and the change starts with the way you see your life and the direction it's taking. As much as I hate to say it, Generations X and Y seem to be choosing to live their lives on green – seeking quick

Life Is Like A Traffic Light

and instantaneous gratification. They find it difficult to still themselves and find their own way; instead, they'd rather seek direction from an influencer on social media than develop their own path.

If you want to be different you must first *think* differently – and set yourself apart from the crowd. Leaders tend to be focused visionaries setting their own trends. Are you a leader or the led? The best advice in this regard is to find your lane, anticipate the road ahead and navigate your own path. Begin looking at your life's progression and the stages as they relate to the indicators of the traffic light. The basic and elementary rules assigned to each of the colors can be a signal or alarm to help navigate your path. I truly believe the awareness of where we've been is pivotal in choosing where we want to go and the road we choose to follow.

Life Is Like A Traffic Light

The Meaning of Yellow light

Slow down.
Think before acting.
Wait for the right time.
Gain control.
Unhurried.

Life Is Like A Traffic Light

The Yellow Light

In the game "Green light, Red light," there were no yellow lights. The game was about go and stop. There was no "slow down and think."

However, we all need a little yellow in our lives. We need to slow down and gather our thoughts to find the right balance. Going, going, going or stopping and being still without any movement (at least for too long) is not good for anyone.

When the rabbit raced the turtle and the turtle won, it wasn't because the turtle was faster than the rabbit. The turtle won the race because he took his time and thought about how he could win the race by being smart, not fast. The turtle got a chance to smell the roses, see the landscape, watch the other animals play and make discoveries along the way. It's hard for an

Life Is Like A Traffic Light

Indy 500 car going 200 miles per hour see a deer eating from a tree or a butterfly landing on a log.

As you age or mature you usually find yourself moving at a slower pace. You're no longer in a hurry to get where you're going. You figure, "I'll get there soon enough and safely." Besides missing the little things along the way, moving too fast can endanger yourself and/or others. Our lives are a product of the decisions we make. You can decide to speed up and go through the yellow light, hoping the red light doesn't catch you, but why take that chance? The yellow light is just as important, if not more, important than green and red.

As we did in the Green chapter, let's take a moment to reflect on a few of the concepts that the color <u>Yellow</u> is associated with: **Happiness**, **Optimism**, **Enlightenment** and **Creativity**.

Life Is Like A Traffic Light

HAPPINESS

What is Happiness? This is a question millions of people have asked themselves or seek to discover over the years. Some find temporary glimmers of happiness in external things such as: buying a big house, a nice car, fancy clothes or having lots of followers on social media. True happiness cannot be reduced to material possessions or "likes" simply because the thrill of a new thing quickly dissipates with the desire for the next and social media relationships tend to be shallow. This is why so find it difficult to maintain happiness in this way. They are seeking happiness in the wrong places and in the wrong things.

I realized in 2008 that true happiness was having the ability to come and go as I pleased or having choices when it comes to simple thing like food or having that one special person that you can call your tangible true friend and

Life Is Like A Traffic Light

certainly not one gained through a "Friend request." Love is also a part of happiness. When love is in your heart, it impacts the soul and everything and person around you benefits. Love is an equalizer and protector. When in love and being loved there not much that can divide, bring you down or disrupt your pursuit of happiness.

OPTIMISM

Slowing down and easing into the yellow gives us the ability to develop **Optimism** toward our path. It gives us an opportunity to not only dream of doing something, but to believe it can be done. It adds a little Green to your life. Yellow optimism is saying, "Go do what you believe you can do, regardless of the possibility of failure." If you look at every failure as an attempt and every attempt was something you believed in, then it's not a failure. It becomes a reminder of your

Life Is Like A Traffic Light

mistakes and how to do it better the next time. The stigma that has been placed on the word "failure" has caused so many people to be afraid to believe and try new things – whether it be a new career, hobby or relationship. Bring a little yellow into your life and believe that you have the chance to have and do so much more.

ENLIGHTENMENT

When you start to think in the yellow and put green and red in the back of your thoughts, you will find that you're able to discover the true awareness of all that lies inside you. *Enlightenment* brings a whole new meaning to living. You start to see things clearly because you reduce your speed. Things you once had a problem understanding seem reasonable and no longer confusing. Your awareness will awaken your inner spirit and teach you how to focus on being happy with yourself. When you start to

Life Is Like A Traffic Light

move at a steady pace, you're able to pay better attention and fill your mind with the wisdom that those who came before you readily offer. You will find yourself seeking and absorbing knowledge because you are now able to hear and process information clearly within the period of enlightenment.

CREATIVITY

How could living in the yellow really make a difference? In this space of being still and relaxing, the creative process has room to flourish. Your imagination starts to blossom and ideas start to flow. You become motivated to make things happen and you realize how short life is, even if you're still in your early years. You no longer want to follow people who aren't going where you're trying to go. You become an originator rather than a copier. Your individuality starts to shine and others will see

Life Is Like A Traffic Light

the change in you without your ever saying a single word. You will become inspired and your vision clear. You can see how much time you have wasted in your life—the time you gave others that, perhaps, was never appreciated. You will put *yourself* first.

In the literal sense of the traffic light, yellow gets little respect because we don't see it as a true call for action. It is neither "stop" nor "go" and seemingly gives the choice to proceed as we see fit. We forget that its importance lies in the caution it wields – the reminder to be alert and ensure the path, whatever that may be, is clear.

In the same way, we shouldn't ignore the important stage in life that pausing in yellow can provide. Here, things may be more stable – you're no longer chasing, but maintaining. You may be here a while or find yourself falling forward or back into green or red.

As things change in the world and in our lives,

Life Is Like A Traffic Light

we must learn to adapt and pivot. For example, the 2019 Coronavirus pandemic forced many to change course in ways they would never have anticipated. Individuals and businesses alike were forced to re-evaluate and prioritize various aspects of everyday life. Safety became the 1st priority and necessity became the motivation. Those who slowed and pivoted often fared better than those who kept in the green and refused to adjust to the new norm. Maintaining life in the yellow can feel mundane but, in my opinion, the greatest opportunity for self-reflection and prioritization of what truly matters is in this slow and content space of life. This is where the lessons of life become vivid and the necessary tools we need to change course are harnessed. Learning discipline and delaying gratification are essential.

A young boy was in a place where his life seemed to be on hold, and when he entered the

Life Is Like A Traffic Light

green zone couldn't stop. After a few years, he found himself back in the ghetto after greed have overtaken him and landed him in federal prison. When our focus is on excess we lose our gauge for what is truly enough. No yellow or red zone in sight. Everything is green. If we only gave equal respect to all three of life's traffic signals, we might better protect ourselves and others financially, emotionally and physically.

    The signs and urges to live a healthy and balanced lifestyle are constantly showing up and seeking our attention, if only we acknowledge them. There are so many ways to receive messages that can help guide or redirect our paths – a Sunday sermon, lyrics from a song, a photographic or TV image....it goes on and on. Those examples require hearing beyond listening and seeing beyond looking, whereas the traffic light is strictly your own measure and gauge based on your own life's experiences. You

Life Is Like A Traffic Light

decide what the changing of the lights mean to you and your response to them. Just as life around us is in a constant state of change so are we physically and mentally. Some changes will be slow and subtle other obvious and rapid. Fearing and running from change will not keep it from happening. How well we manage the ups and downs will determine the frequency of green, yellow and red light experiences.

My own mistakes and the lessons I've learned from them have shaped me into the person I am today. I no longer feel I need to have the latest and greatest anything. At age sixty-two I have finally realized that yellow has become one of my favorite colors by far.

To my younger self and to today's youth: Consider pros and cons before you act. Listen before you speak. It's okay to say "no" and "I don't know." Don't be quick to follow any group or way of thinking. Ask many questions and

Life Is Like A Traffic Light

seek counsel when needed. You owe that much to yourself. Slow down and plan your life. Stop living only for today rather than the years to come. Life is worth more than 24 hours of fun. Reduce the mistakes in your life by taking a breath in yellow to learn from others. Every move should be calculated. Your positive is your profit, your negative is your loss, so figure out what your gain is. Find your balance in life. Be happy with the little things and thankful for the plenty.

Life Is Like A Traffic Light

The Meaning of Red light

Stop.

Stuck.

Lack of motivation.

Giving up.

Life Is Like A Traffic Light

The Red Light

Now we come to the final light – and the most nuanced of them all. The red zone could serve as the place we start from or a place that we fall back into after suffering some losses in yellow or green. Whatever the season of life we're in, the one thing we all must keep in mind is that red is always in existence – it doesn't go away just because you currently live in a yellow or green light space.

In some cases, a red-light experience can be a lifesaver for someone going too fast and spending too much time in the green. For example, a career executive who has been climbing the corporate ladder and burning the candle at both ends for many years may be well served by a life-changing circumstance that lands them back in the red so that they can shift

Life Is Like A Traffic Light

focus on what truly matters. Being forced to stop and retreat from the rat race of life could provide an opportunity for reflection.

We often forget how important it is to unplug, reflect and reset. So many external things vie for our attention. Careers, family responsibilities, social events and the constant influx of information pumping through emails, text messaging, social and tv media have us moving and reacting constantly. Finding the time to stop and reset can be a challenge. When we do take a pause for a meal or rest, our brains are still teeming with the anxiety and stress of what remains undone. What if you schedule a stop or pause once a week, just for one hour to reflect on the present, your life's direction and whether your actions are in line with your goals? This time could make all the difference in how you navigate through life. When in the red zone it should be all about you. You need to be satisfied

Life Is Like A Traffic Light

with the choices you made in life.
"Stopping" in many senses of the word can be beneficial to both the individual and society. If families *stopped* consuming so many processed foods and overeating there would be much less obesity. If people *stopped* smoking it would reduce the rates of cancer or lung disease. If drivers *stopped* rushing on their commute fewer accidents would occur. If teens *stopped* having unprotected sex there would be less teen pregnancy, fatherless children and sexually transmitted diseases. If addicts *stopped* abusing drugs there would be a lessor need for rehabilitation centers, homelessness and crime. If people *stopped* letting fear control their thoughts, many more would achieve their goals and many more dreams would manifest. If we *stopped* blaming others for our life's setbacks, more self-healing and development could occur. If we *stopped* to smell the roses and take a hard

Life Is Like A Traffic Light

look at our life, one could see so many reasons to be grateful for the opportunities that exist.

Changing lights can be a difficult transition for anyone. For example, let's say that, after many years of working in a corporate environment, adhering to an imposed culture, hierarchy and maneuvering within the political confines, you one day achieve the goal of starting your own company and becoming your own boss. Once you're the boss, the standard and rules are set by you. The transition of your light will take time and will require a change in mindset and discipline for the transition to be successful. You will have to learn to think like a boss. Stop (red).... contemplate (yellow).... pivot (go). The transition from employee to boss can be just as daunting as it is exciting. Proceeding with small strategic steps help in maintaining the course. However, sudden uncalculated moves can result in varying negative outcomes

Life Is Like A Traffic Light

that can drain your motivation and drive. Realistically, the road to becoming one's own boss is paved with detours, roadblocks and forks in the road. Anticipating setbacks and learning how and when to pivot are crucial. Not everyone has the fortitude to embark on that journey. Many individuals with great ideas, skills and abilities play it safe. They live and find contentment in yellow and even red. Fear of failure and unwillingness to make the necessary sacrifices keeps them in what can be described as a dead end job or situation. They will often talk about concepts and ideas.... throw around "if I could, I would" stories but never pull the trigger or step on the gas. However, those that take that leap of faith and answer the call inside them become transformed in a way that only those with a similar experience can understand. That's why it's of major importance that those considering such a transition surround

Life Is Like A Traffic Light

themselves with like-minded individuals. These people can mentor, encourage, support, offer guidance, connection etc. along the way. So, when considering a transition, the plan needs to take into consideration the ups, downs and network of players on the road. Begin with the end goal in mind and never lose sight of the colors in your pathway.

There is a time and a place in your life when it's good to find your red zone and stop. For example, after working hard for 32 years you decide to finally retire. Here it may be good to stop and pivot to find a project or hobby to fill your days with purpose.

Perhaps you picked up a gambling habit and have lost more dollars than you can count, your family and or your home. You may find it useful to sit in red to contemplate your losses and rehabilitate.

Sometimes you may not be given the choice

Life Is Like A Traffic Light

to stop on your own. Life itself may find a way to stop you in your tracks. When life decides to stop you, it may disrupt your entire life. Take this true story for example. There were three young boys growing up in a tough (in every sense of the word) neighborhood. None of the boys had a father figure in their lives and grew up in single parent household. One day the boys decided to sell drugs. Their plan was to sell drugs for a short period of time. One of the boys wanted to make enough money to help his mother put a down payment on a home. The second boy desired to buy his mother a car so she wouldn't have to take public transportation at night to go to work. The last boy wanted to make enough money to start his own business.

Six months later, all three boys made enough money to do exactly what they set out to do. So, the time came to stop, as planned. All three had reached the point of contentment

Life Is Like A Traffic Light

according to the goals they had set at the start. They were lucky. They ventured down a dark road and avoided all negative consequences. Nobody was arrested or lost their life. They were all free to resume their lives with a feeling of accomplishment. However, as the story goes, one of the boys decided to *not* stop. He wasn't ready to retreat to his red zone. Because the hustle came easy to him and he loved the options the selling life afforded, he decided this was better and, at the time, worth the risk. He somehow believed he was invincible and didn't see (or chose to ignore) all the flashing lights on the horizon. His crew could not convince him to stick to the plan. It was exactly thirty-seven days later that the boy was robbed and shot five times, leaving him paralyzed from the neck down. The incident instantaneously catapulted him into the red zone, with his life forever changed.

I'm sure there are tens of thousands of stories

Life Is Like A Traffic Light

like this one that go untold. As I stated earlier in this book, I too have made mistakes and have a few regrets. I have come to realize that many of my mistakes resulted from not wanting to listen or take advice from others. When we were children, we had parent(s) to teach us the difference between wrong and right. They set the boundaries. Once an adult, we tend to create our own set of rules and leave parental guidance behind. We govern ourselves, establish our own boundaries and, if we're not careful, fall into undesirable situations of our own making. Ignoring the signs, not listening to advice and dismissing our own gut feelings are acts that can contribute to one's demise.

Why would one choose red or take a risk that may result in red? Could it be its just human and in our blood to take risk? I say it's not. We're not born to do wrong; these behaviors are picked up along the road of life. We put into practice

Life Is Like A Traffic Light

what we hear and see. We know when the light turns red it means stop but we are conditioned to rationalize and find reasons to go right on through. Why is it easy to start something but so much harder to stop? Is it because we believe that if we stop we will be missing out? We gave up too soon? Or is it the feeling you get when you've gotten away with something? Out of all the reasons, I believe it's the feeling of excitement that motivates us to act out. It's important to be aware when something is good *to* you but not good *for* you. That mere awareness could make the difference in *knowing* when to stop something and *actually* stopping.

When you use the "stops" in your life to be a stage of growth and awareness – the outcome can be so rewarding.

- **Stop and dream.** Usually when we are still we can relax and quiet our minds. This is

Life Is Like A Traffic Light

when your dreams can come through and become clear to you.
- **Stop and be happy.** When you're able to put everything on hold and stop everything, including your thoughts, it allows you to choose happy thoughts and that joy is contagious.
- **Stop and love**. When we decide to stop moving so fast we can find the time to love. When we're moving too fast, we can miss out on love.

When we think of the traffic light colors metaphorically, they come to mean so much more than go, slow down or stop. Hopefully, the next time you come to a traffic light you'll be reminded to take a moment and evaluate where your life is at. Maybe the green will motivate you to start a project that you've been pitting off. Or if you feel like you're caught in the

Life Is Like A Traffic Light

hamster wheel of life, the yellow may urge you to slow down and press your re-start button. Stopping and slowing allows for clarity. You come to terms with what's important to you and appreciate the simple pleasures. We must stop and assess where we are, where we are going and who we want to go with. If we're not satisfied with the answers to those questions, it may be time to start working on ourselves, adjust or pivot our plans and clear out any relationships that are not in line with what we want for ourselves. Remember, for the traffic light concept to work *all* the signals must be acknowledged and respected. *You* are in the driver's seat. *You* are responsible. What needs to be done is in *your* hands. And as you tread on the road you must be aware that you're not alone. You share the road with many others that are on different paths and in various stages of red, yellow and green of their own. Our

Life Is Like A Traffic Light

paths are constantly merging and crossing with those operating in all the different stages. The awareness that not everyone is where you are can make all the difference in how we move through life.

Empathy and awareness could influence your responses and reactions with those you encounter. For example, when you see an elderly person moving slowly as they cross the street, your awareness and empathy may trigger you to want to help. You may come to appreciate the differences in the culture, race and language of others. Maybe you now are interested in learning more about them. Maybe you realize that you have more in common than not.

Opening your mind and heart and operating in a space of awareness and empathy can open many opportunities to learn and grow. These experiences can be life changing and offer fulfillment that nothing can buy.

Life Is Like A Traffic Light

When I set out to write this book, I wanted to create an accessible metaphor to help guide people on all walks of life safely through their journey. Today, I'm no longer the only advisor in my life. I seek and listen to those who I respect and love. I compile all pertinent facts then make my best-informed decision and/or choices.
I feel compelled to share the mistakes I made in my life with anyone who might benefit from them. The wheel doesn't have to be reinvented, but it *can* be improved. Obviously not everyone will heed the lessons bestowed upon them. If one is not ready to receive it, the knowledge will fall by the wayside.

When I look at some of the choices that our youths make, seemingly without much regard for consequences, it fires my desire to share and enlighten. Watching from afar, shaking my head and doing nothing began to erode my conscience. So, writing this short book is one

Life Is Like A Traffic Light

of the ways I choose to give back and hopefully reach those who are open to receiving my words.

No one goes through life without experiencing all the stages of the traffic light. So it's best we develop the coping tools and perspective to maneuver. Having experienced all the colors at one time or another can equip you with the balance needed to function and take something valuable from each stage.

Create your own Traffic Light Chart by drawing three circles and following the instructions below:

> **Green:** In this circle, write a start and end date for whatever you're planning to start doing. Your end date should be your goal.
>
> **Yellow:** In this circle, evaluate your progress. This is also the time to make changes. Re-think your plan or start over, if need be.
>
> **Red**: In this circle, write the word "Stop."

Life Is Like A Traffic Light

Review what stage you're in. Are things going as planned? Don't be afraid to stop and start over. Stopping doesn't mean failure. Starting over should be expected and it's an act of strength and faith.

Creating the chart will help you make your plan and visualize your goals. The chart should be your guide and serve as inspiration.

This guide can be used over and over as you set and conquer new goals. For certainly as it has been said "if you fail to plan, you plan to fail."

In business or life itself, know when to start and when to stop. Faith, not fear, is what should drive the car. Having passion and patience will keep you motivated. None of the lights are truly negative or positive, it's all in your perception. You made the plan, you change the plan....you are in control.

Life Is Like A Traffic Light

Life Is Like A Traffic Light is to be used as a basic tool. It isn't meant to provide you with answers or predict the future or make any guarantees. The concept is meant to be relatable and a simple way to view our path. On my own path to my 60s, I experienced my share of red, yellow and green lights. The cycle is inevitable, but we can control how we respond and what we learn during the different stages. Each stage serves as a chance to sharpen our coping skills. Eventually, the transitioning through the highs and lows will become less jolting and more manageable. Our past successes and failures provide an awesome opportunity to grow and elevate towards our goals.

The universe has its way of nudging us in the way we should go. It's up us to be aware and allow the flow to occur in our lives.

Keep these three colors on your mind at all times. When you're going through something,

Life Is Like A Traffic Light

use one or all three colors to gain perspective. If you're feeling down or have a bad day, use the colors yellow and red to slow down, stop and reflect, then use the color green to motivate yourself to get up, shake it off move forward.

Signs that can define where you are and what you do.
- The **Yield** can have you thinking you reached your peak in life and it's the end of the road for you.
- The **Detour** will redirect your path and force you to find another route to your destination, which can make the road to getting there longer or shorter.
- The **Merge** will have things intersecting into one, forcing everything to fit, which could later cause unnecessary pressure.
- The **Bumps** indicate there will be turmoil. Nothing is easy.
- The **Warning** tells of danger ahead and you must

Life Is Like A Traffic Light

prepare to deal with the unknown.
- The **Caution** is a heads-up. We need to proceed carefully and calculatingly.
- The **Emergency Exit** shows a way to go in case of an unexpected occurrence. You should always be aware of a way to exit.
- The **Keep Right** means there are no options for you, there's only one way to proceed.
- The **No U-Turn** is a clear indicator of no turning back. You must proceed regardless.
- The **Stop Sign** can only be translated as stop. No matter the current plans or activity it all must stop.

In life we have choices. We can choose to obey or ignore the signs. That choice is most often an opportunity to make a decision that could reshape our entire life for better or worse. This is why it's important for us to be aware of the signals – so that when the time comes to react, we're ready.

Life Is Like A Traffic Light

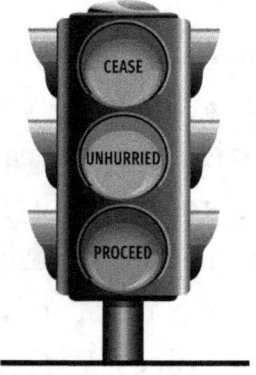

Life Is Like a Traffic Light;

be prepared for change.

Life Is Like A Traffic Light

Green represents:

Growth

Life Is Like A Traffic Light

Spiritually, the color **Green** represents:

New Beginnings

Hope

Peace

Life Is Like A Traffic Light

Green also symbolizes:

Good Luck
Health
Tranquility

Life Is Like A Traffic Light

Green personality traits:

Perfectionist
Analytical
Logical

Life Is Like A Traffic Light

Yellow represents:

Happiness

Life Is Like A Traffic Light

Spiritually, the color **Yellow** represents:

Self-Confidence

Courage

Fulfilment

Life Is Like A Traffic Light

Yellow also symbolizes:

Positivity
Optimism
Loyalty

Life Is Like A Traffic Light

Yellow personality traits:

Enthusiasm
Verbally Articulate
Creative

Life Is Like A Traffic Light

Red represents:

Passionate Love

Life Is Like A Traffic Light

Spiritually, the color **Red** represents:

Power

Action

Life Is Like A Traffic Light

Red also symbolizes:

Emotions

Strength

Danger

Life Is Like A Traffic Light

Red personality traits:

Decisive

Assertive

Honest

Life Is Like A Traffic Light

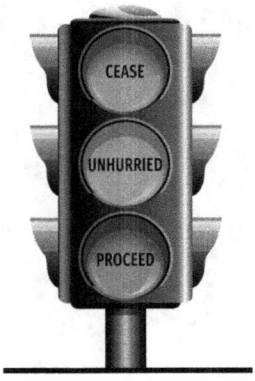

Life Is Like a Traffic Light

Life Is Like A Traffic Light

www.ingramcontent.com/pod-product-compliance
Lightning Source LLC
Chambersburg PA
CBHW071253070526
44583CB00017B/2451